FALLING INTO THE SKY

FALLING INTO THE SKY

A Meditation Anthology

ABHI JANAMANCHI
ABHIMANYU JANAMANCHI

EDITORS

SKINNER HOUSE BOOKS

BOSTON

www.skinnerhouse.org

Printed in the United States

Cover design by Kathryn Sky-Peck
Text design by Suzanne Morgan
Cover photograph "Toward Heaven" © Cathleen Tarawhiti

print ISBN: 978-1-55896-694-9
eBook ISBN: 978-1-55896-695-6

6 5 4 3 2 1
15 14 13

"Falling into the Sky" by David Breeden was previously published in *Blue Lyra Review*.

"Hidden in the Heart" by Karen Hering was previously published by Wisdom Ways Center for Spirituality, St. Paul, Minnesota, in its Fall 2010 catalog.

Library of Congress Cataloging-in-Publication Data

Falling into the sky : a meditation anthology / Abhi and Abhimanyu Janamanchi, editors.
        pages cm
  ISBN 978-1-55896-694-9 (pbk. : alk. paper)—
ISBN 978-1-55896-695-6 (ebook) 1. Meditations. 2. Spiritual life—Unitarian Universalist churches—Meditations.
I. Janamanchi, Abhi. II. Janamanchi, Abhimanyu.
  BX9855.F35 2013
  242—dc23
                                    2012041821

CONTENTS

What is Unitarian Universalist spirituality? One answer lies in the familiar Zen story about a monk who was being chased by a tiger. In his haste, the monk trips and falls off a cliff. As he hangs from a branch for dear life, he notices another tiger circling at the bottom, ready to catch him when he falls. And then he sees a mouse gnawing away at the branch to which he clings. At that very moment, the monk sees a wonderfully luscious strawberry hanging off a shrub on the side. He picks the strawberry, pops it in his mouth, and savors the taste. UU spirituality is about living fully in the moment and living it as if it were our last.

For Unitarian Universalists, the spiritual is not just sequestered in churches, temples, or monasteries. It is an integral part of our lives, of our thoughts and actions, and impels us to live lives of joy, hope, and service. While we cannot avoid or escape the daily tigers that encircle the mind and soul, we can, like the monk in the parable, appreciate and savor the preciousness of each moment as if it were our last. For, who knows? It might be the only strawberry we'll ever eat.

This is where *Falling Into the Sky* provides a treasure trove of contemplative tranquility, a sanctuary of the spirit where we can find strength and hope to face the daily challenges of our lives. The authors of these prayers, meditations, and short essays are Unitarian Universalist ministers and lay people, theologians and poets, philosophers and activists. Each of them provides a personal insight into the workings of the inner self and how we might be able to accede to a realm where calm has replaced busy-ness, peace has overcome anxiety, and compassion has delivered the soul from selfishness. Each reminds us that meditation, like Unitarian Universalism, can come in many forms and is ultimately about being grounded and fully present in the moment.

May you be well, calm, happy, and peaceful.

Abhi Janamanchi

Abhimanyu Janamanchi

FALLING INTO THE SKY

Based on a Poem by Zen Monk Muso Soseki

I dug and dug
Deeper into the earth

Looking for blue heaven
Choking always

On piles of dust rising

Then once
At midnight
I slipped

And fell into the sky

DAVID BREEDEN

JOY

I have been wondering
what the morning glories
know. Is it envy
that compels these vines
to strangle other flowers
arising in their path?

Or perhaps self-preservation,
to climb these walls, forsaking
humbler beings, winding
greedy stems around the trellis
in their hungry pursuit of light.

Still, every morning,
basking in their spiral shadows,
I want to believe it is something more

this fevered yearning
to open purple flowers,
yield bold-throated *Glorias*
to the sun,
and in the blaze of afternoon
curl petals softly into shyness.

And every morning, I plead
with the dew-moist buds
to know their secret joy:

to open and close without holding,
to surrender all to light,
to sing
I am completely yours
over and over again.

TERRI PAHUCKI

MORE THAN A CUP OF SOUP

Not far from where I work there is a little hole-in-the-wall café, a good place to pick up a quick lunch. You have to be in the mood for soup, however, because all this place ever serves is soup, accompanied by a homemade bread roll. You also have to be feeling open-minded and flexible, because there is only one kind of soup made fresh each day, though sometimes you can also have yesterday's soup at a reduced price.

The woman who works behind the counter always looks glad to be there, doing what she's doing, and she often knows her customers by name. Last week there were at least a half-dozen people waiting in line to be served, but she still lingered with an old man at the counter who already had his soup and bread in a paper bag. She asked after his health and then asked about his wife. She commiserated with him when he told her about their illnesses. When she said goodbye, she touched his hand lightly, smiled into his face, and told him she'd look for him tomorrow. It was a wonderful thing just then, to be marooned on this little island of calm amidst the impatience, irritability, and general craziness of life, in a place where someone makes her living by patiently shaping and then serving two of the world's most basic and nourishing foods.

It can't be an easy way to make a living, and it's surely no way to get rich. But there is serenity in the woman's face and a gentleness in her voice when she invites you to make the one simple choice available there: butter roll or rye? Watching her at work, it's easy to believe that some small corner of the world's fabric is being patiently, lovingly stitched back together—and that something more gets carried out the door than a bag of bread and warm soup.

KATHLEEN McTIGUE

OUT OF SEASON

A flash of purple out of season
A clutch of tiny crocuses
Caught in rhyme without a reason
But my need to mark their time.

Pushing out of dark security
Bent and curled against the cold
Untimely beauty here and gone
Their too short story told.

Just days ago, too warm for winter
Seemed far more like May
So, crocuses,
Who do not heed
Our ordered Roman plan
Of day and week
Responded only as they can
And grew.

Today,
The tiny purple masses quiver
Shiver, in a cruel, still winter wind
In sunshine false and cold as charity.
And then I see
With perfect clarity
This flash of purple out of season
Caught in rhyme
Without a reason

Other than their need to be
Is a parable that's meant for me.

That beauty really is its own reward
That best laid plans
With charted graphs and demarcations
Foolish bold prognostications
Hold nothing of the mystery
I see
Within this flower out of season
Or so I thought
. . . until I thought.
For everything . . . there really is a reason.

JUDITH CAMPBELL

THE REDWOOD

A few years ago, I went camping alone at Pfeiffer-Big Sur State Park. I set up my light-weight tent at the base of a giant redwood and cooked dinner over a camp fire. It was growing dark and cool. The campground sounds of voices, children playing, dogs, were quieting down. I doused the fire and crawled into the tent, into my sleeping bag, and put my ear to the ground.

Be still now. . . . Be still now.

I heard, down through the earth, the roots of the redwood strain and groan. Up above, way up that massive trunk, the tree must have been swaying in the starlit night, however gently, with the wind. And I, who could not see the movement above ground, could hear, below ground, the roots reaching toward the center of the earth. I could hear the roots hanging on, holding steady, keeping center, giving and taking.

I was unforgettably spoken to by this voice from deep below ground, the song of the redwood roots. The tree ceased to be an "It," and the tree and I vibrated together in the dark, somewhere below language. In the "Thou" I said to the tree, I somehow addressed the eternal Thou—that interdependent web of all existence. In the groaning of the roots, I heard the song of the universe.

JEANNE FOSTER

APRIL MORNING WORSHIP

A gentle haze hovered as we walked the stretch of quiet beach. Cool not cold, the wisp of mist an open-weave blanket around my shoulders. Willy walked along, sometimes stopping to sniff or pee, or running a little ahead but not too far.

Soul and place and pace became a single flow of person, dog, and time. "Archetypal," I thought. "Or is it is primordial?" Woman and dog, beach and silence, mist and wonder. Connected to the ground of my being, I felt peace.

Then I remembered. It is Sunday morning. Actually, 10:30 Sunday morning—worship time. I am not in church.

Off from preaching, recovering from jet lag, I had decided to sleep in. Yet I had not missed church at all. It was with me on the beach in the stillness and the quiet, where I was greeted as if God knew we have a date every Sunday morning. Location mattered not. God was there, as God always is. And God or grace made sure I was too.

ANITA FARBER-ROBERTSON

ASCENSION

Despite brown edges,
we can count on the dogwood,
count on the azaleas,
on irises and morning glories.
They are our resurrection,
rising to meet the season,
no matter how muddy or disconsolate.
We can depend on their ascension,
a private Easter
poking through the clay soil,
count on what's been planted
to merit praise and glory.
Hallelujah! Each bloom and tendril.

MARTI KELLER

BLACK ANTS

Many years ago we lived in an apartment that had its share of domestic wildlife—squirrels and raccoons lived in the attic, mice in the walls.

Our kitchen was home to black ants. I tried to deter them in unsuccessful, non-toxic ways and would sweep them away or step on them when I saw them. One day, cleaning up our round kitchen table, I saw a black ant perched near the edge. I raised my hand to sweep it off when I realized that the ant was cleaning its face and antennae just like my cats, stroking its antennae like a miniature black panther. This kinship with my beloved cats astonished me, and I sat on a chair and watched the ant for at least five minutes. Black, with a not-quite-glossy sheen, delicate legs and antennae, the ant was gorgeous.

In the days after, I watched the ants trundle around the countertops, gently shooing them out of the way, lifting them out of places I didn't want them. If they fell in the sink as I did the dishes, I fished them out and set them curled up on the counter; after a time, during which I was sure they were dead, they would stretch out and shake off the water, and wander off. Ant resurrection!

I haven't intentionally hurt an ant since.

FIONA HEATH

PLOTTING ON RURAL ROUTE ONE

If we were to meet again in April
what else would we do
but tromp your boggy woods,
me in borrowed boots, and look for herons,
or walk the rural route, now paved,
in search of shared memories,
repurposing our lives.

MARTI KELLER

SILENCE IN THE PRAYER CIRCLE

Moving wind,
bending branches,
shining leaves
are speech enough
this afternoon.
Water ripples in granite
where finches bathe and drink.
The bay beyond glitters and,
closer by, the largest tree
spreads nearly naked arms.
A sudden bird
speaks for us all,

each of us in solitary
solidarity, our lives unspoken,
already known to each other.
We need no more word
than the three-lobed leaf
still clinging to the peony
stem, drinking life
from what is left,
like us.

KAREN LEWIS FOLEY

CARRIED UP TO BED

Wouldn't we all wish to be carried up to bed one more time?

So dependent, so confident, and so cared for, in that particular way, for all the right reasons. We are not ill, nor hurt, nor helpless. We are simply small and tender and tired.

How long have parents carried their children to bed, while children enjoy that passive bliss? There we lie, half-asleep already, in a car or on a sofa after a late night. We could be roused but our eyes are closed. We are less asleep than we look, more asleep than we feel.

Our parent comes to fetch us up to bed and slides a strong, quiet arm under our shoulders and neck, another under our knees, and hoists us up to be carried to our rooms and our waiting sheets. We sleepily turn toward them, maybe hike an arm loosely over their shoulder and around their neck and hang on a bit. We feel them walking down the hall, or stepping up the stairs, then nudging open the door, walking across the floor of the dark, familiar space. We know where we are without opening our eyes. We feel them pause by the bed to get a firmer grip, and then lean over and lay us down, adjusting the sheets to tuck us in.

Would that I had known that last time for what it was. Now it is my task to do the tender carry, the kiss and caress before leaving the room. That is precious too. But, children, know the date-stamped preciousness of being carried up to bed for what it is and nestle into its warmth.

Years will pass and we will still feel small and tender and tired and this gift will likewise have passed, gone to others, to our own and others' children. And we will each of us have then only the memory and the charge to carry on the tradition, the sweet burden, the carrying of another.

ELIZABETH LERNER MACLAY

FOR A SWEET MINUTE

Now the trees sway. Now
the long-awaited rain. Now
a great blue heron standing
unmoving minute after minute
on a log at pond's edge.
Now a human watching
the heron, the trees, the
long awaited rain. Now
two pileated woodpeckers
flapping across the pond
up and up to bare vertical
branches of the tallest tree.
Four living creatures
and these living plants.
Dots in a cosmos.
Are we connected?
The heron dives,
comes out with a frog,
adjusts the frog, swallows.
The woodpeckers fly away.
I go inside. Perhaps for that
sweet minute we were together.

JOAN McINTOSH

BEYOND BORDERS

Go forth
Because we are always going forth from
    somewhere

Going from our homes, our childhoods
Going from our cities and countries
Going from innocence to experience to
    enlightenment

Going into mystery and questions
Going into the desert
Getting to the other side.

Go forth,
Leave behind the comfort and community
    of one place
Head into the anxiety and loneliness of another.

Carry with you the love and laughter of this place
And let it light your way
Carry with you the wisdom you learned
and the good memories
May they give you strength for your journey

And when you have been away long enough,
    far enough,
Done what you'd set off to do

Been there so long
That place too, starts to feel like home

Come back
Come back to the one, universal
Everywhere and every when and everyone
    inclusive home,
This beloved community of all creation
That you can never really leave.

RICK HOYT

MORNING MEDITATION

A buzz and smatter—
images and words swim
unbidden, pulling you into
a bright current, but you

want the dark and silent place
beneath water's pull,
that space under your heart
beyond Orion, the Pleiades.

And if you stay on this couch,
chair, mat, and do not move
and sense the candle flame
in the gathering gray light

you may slip unbidden
(yet you're sure you worked for it),
drop into depth, the place
unearned, as it always is,

bottomless, yielding.
Consciousness may hold you.
You know this always, sitting,
treading water, trying not to wait.

KAREN LEWIS FOLEY

WITHIN THE LIGHT

Headlights, taillights, going, coming;
it does not matter inside.
Draw a curtain across the window,
lock the door and break the key.
Let the interior deepen and broaden
until it exceeds this little room.
You will go out when you are ready,
when the tiny inner Self no longer fits.
Awareness will come, yet bliss is not the goal:
pure consciousness, a word to the stranger
become friend, that is All.

JEAN M. OLSON

SPIRIT OF THE FALLS

A spirit once dwelt here, manifest in the rock that
    guides the water.
A spirit dwelt here once, alive in the trees and plants,
holding back the dirt, keeping the mountain from
    sliding to the river.

A spirit dwelt here once,
I felt it as a child, visiting this place and playing
in the spray of the falls.
I felt the spirit in that mist, playing with me,
dancing and laughing as I danced and laughed.
It walked the hidden trails, following me
as I made my way in search of hidden treasures:
a growth of moss in an artful space,
a purple flower at the base of the hill,
the crooked branches of a tree, reaching
for a space in the sun.

A spirit dwelt here, once.
I search for it now, along the paved trails,
amid the people and noise.
I strain to find it in the mist of the falls.
I seek it in the hidden treasures,
I look for it in the air,
sit and wait
for all else to disappear.

A spirit still dwells here, somewhere
beyond the many feet moving quickly on established
    trails.
A spirit dwells here still, past the barricade at the
    water's edge,
laughing and dancing, at a distance.
A spirit dwells here, still among the purple flowers,
sprouting in sheltered silence beyond the weather-
    worn logs.
A spirit dwells here still, in the million shades
    of green,
growing on branches forever searching
for the sun.

A spirit dwells here, still,
and longs for a time
long before the time
when I found comfort in its essence.

ALLISON C. GAMMONS

BARUCH ATAH ILLINOIS

Like many UU families, the interfaith Zuckers
attended at least one Passover Seder every Spring.
We also lit Hanukkah candles each December on
Grandma Esther's hand-me-down Menorah. Ritu-
als for both holidays include the traditional Jewish
prayers, which begin: "Baruch atah Adonai . . . "
(Blessed art thou, O Lord . . .). Many Seders ago,
my then-nine-year-old daughter Michaela, who has
been known to charmingly fracture many a phrase,
intoned clear and loud as a bell "Baruch atah Illinois
. . ." (Blessed art thou, Illinois . . .). Needless to say,
we all laughed ourselves silly!

It is amusing, though, to ponder whether the
Prairie State might actually be more sacred than,
say, the Buckeye State, the Pine Tree State, the Show-
Me State, the Gopher State, or the Mass Bay Colony.
But it isn't. *Sacred space* is where you find it, where
you feel grounded and at home and blessed. No pun
intended, but it's a "state of mind," so to speak.

Yes, Illinois is surely the Promised Land for someone, Lake Michigan as holy as the Jordan. But maybe
what *you* consider hallowed ground is that quiet,
shaded corner in your yard where you can inhale
the incense of Spring. It could be that cafe where
you commune with friends over Cabernet and crusty
bread; that Downeast Lake where you exhale a litany

of sighs, or on the front porch swing at Grandma's, gliding back and forth in a rhythm as familiar as an old-time hymn.

So, Blessed art thou, Illinois, Massachusetts, Maine, Ohio, the window seat in the living room, a favorite aisle seat at the movie theater, a sticky bleacher at Fenway, that dependable tree branch, the choir loft at your church, the community hall of your fellowship, the grove at Ferry Beach.

Blessed art thou, all the Chicagos of our hearts, where we feel at home and connected. Blessed art thou, all the sacred spaces, all the Promised Lands, we will create and inhabit together in the days to come.

ROBIN LANDERMAN ZUCKER

MATERIALIZING

In what form did the spirit
appear to you today,
the blossom of a flower,
the tug of a child's hand,
the silent twinkling stars,
an old woman smiling at the bus stop,
a lover's gentle hug,
a presence so close to your soul
you could almost touch it,
words of truth formed
unbidden in your mind?

The holy disguised in so many ways,
may your senses open wide in recognition.

JEAN M. OLSON

WITH EYES THAT SEE

Looking away from my computer screen, my day becomes suddenly arrested by the glory of the maple tree, with its yellow and orange leaves. I see the sun showering it just so. For a moment, it seems to be on fire, the barn beyond it starting to smoke.

I laugh, grateful to be halted from mundane things, jolted into the splendor of the natural world. I pause to express my gratitude. Dropping into my heart, I remind myself that even as I behold this splendor, a more spectacular sight, a greater vision of true art, is to see other people. Unlike the marbled kind that fill museums, the real art—the kind artists strive to imitate—sits peacefully right next to us, or yells in our faces. The real art is in all the shades of skin, all the textures of hair, all the shapes of bodies. Which ones do you notice first?

We see what we want to see and accept into our vision of community what is most familiar. But the true exercise in seeing others as works of art in our communities is to look for who is not there, and should be. When we open our eyes and truly see, we become one with the universal living museum that embraces the beauty of all.

MARTA I. VALENTÍN

A PRAYER FOR UNFINISHED BUSINESS

Dear great lathe of heaven,

O foundry of souls,

You churning, burning cosmos which has wrought
me on the infinite loom of your celestial body.

Spinning stars and indifferent stones: hear my
prayer.

Do not curse me to perish with all my dreams
fulfilled.

Do not afflict me with a vision so narrow and a heart
so small,

That all my greatest hopes could be accomplished
within a single lifetime.

Rather, bless me with an unquiet spirit.

Anoint me with impertinent oils.

Grant me dreams so great and numerous,

That I might spend the fullness of my days to realize
them,

And have ample remaining to leave to my inheritors.

Holy gyre that bore me and must one day take me
home,

Allow me the mercy to depart this life with
unfinished business.

KELLY WEISMAN ASPROOTH-JACKSON

GAIA

I am lush land and rugged rock,
the massive, monumental Mother.
I am the founding force,
the germinating ground.

Touch me,
I am soft as moss and hard as diamond.
I am the soil of the plains,
the sand of the deserts,
the salt of the mountains.
I am forest and canyon,
jungle and tundra,
verdant valley and crystal cavern.

stand on me, I will sustain you.
dig your roots into me, I will nourish you.
grow in my gardens,
feed on my greens,
dance in my meadows,
build from my mud and stone.

I am the abundance of fertile fields,
the beauty of golden lilies,
the sweetness of ripe apples,
the fragrance of myrrh.

I am the rotting vine,
the moldy grain,
the decaying wood.

all matter returns to me,
for I am renewal.
I am the sphere of the seasons.
when your span has ended,
I will bring you home.

JEZIBELL ANAT

MEDITATIONS

1

Wise friend,

words pall and pale before the bounty of your grace
to me.

God grant that I may be of some small solace to you
who leave

me always so richly dowered with joy!

2

Death is the Familiar Stranger whom none can avoid,
no matter

how slick or smart

in the current fashions of this transient world.

Death is only a door

between the cacophony of this world

and the radiant serenity of the next,

where tired souls find respite

before their return

to this passing pageant of

empty pomp and fleeting joys.

SHUMA CHAKRAVARTY

SINFUL

My career in sin began at the First National grocery store in 1961. I was five years old. Coming through the checkout line with my mother, I had this thought about swiping a pack of gum. I knew that I shouldn't, but I also thought that if I asked my mother to buy it, she'd say no. So I waited until the cashier was busy redeeming my mother's coupons, counting out change, and calculating how many S&H green stamps my mother had earned. Then I committed the dirty deed.

For a moment, I was certain that everyone was staring at me. My guilt made me uneasy. I considered putting the gum back. But it was already in my pocket. How would I get the gum out of my pocket and back on the shelf without being noticed? Before I could work out the details, my mother had finished her transaction and was holding out a small bag of groceries for me to carry.

With every step we took toward home, I became more and more worried. What if one of my brothers or sisters asked me where I got it? What if my mother asked me? What would I say? I also started to feel more and more guilty.

Finally, my luck began to turn. A good friend of my mother's was approaching us. Usually when this happened I became very impatient. But this day I was happy to see my mother's friend. As they talked, I slipped the gum into the little green trash container fastened to the streetlight pole. I had never felt so relieved in all my young life.

When we finally got home, my mother thanked me for being patient while she talked with her friend and for carrying the bag of groceries. Her thanking me only made me feel guiltier. Then she told me that as a reward, I could have a piece of the gum she had bought me at the grocery store. Naturally, I thought she meant a pack she had bought on her own—different from the pack of gum. So, I reached out my hand. My mother looked at me oddly and said, "You silly kid! Don't you remember? You put the gum in your trouser pocket." She had obviously seen me take the gum. Or maybe, hmmm . . . yeah, that's it! My mother didn't think I intended to steal the gum at all. She thought that I had made it perfectly obvious to her that I was taking the gum so that she could pay for it.

That day, although I sinned, I felt redeemed by my mother's faith in me. I felt no reason to explain to my mother that I no longer had the gum in my pocket. And she felt no reason to tell me—until many years later—how much she enjoyed the gum after she retrieved it from the little green trash container fastened to the streetlight pole.

BOB McKETCHNIE

GARDEN ZEN

I sit in my garden and contemplate
The depth and profundity of the universe.
And all the while the wind blows gently
From the hills and teases the leaves
And flowers and brushes my hair.
A humming bird visits the bright red sage
And gnats hover in the warm air.

What need is there of profundity
Everything I need is here.

KENNETH COLLIER

GOD'S NAME

God is not God's name
Allah is not Allah's name
Yahweh is not Yahweh's name

Elohim is not Elohim's name
Brahman is not Brahman's name
Mazda is not Mazda's name

Reason is not reason's name
Truth is not truth's name
Multitude is not multitude's name

Names are not names
Naming is not naming
Naming names nothing

DAVID BREEDEN

WITH WHAT KNOWS WHO (GENESIS 32)

Wrestling with the dark,
   with what knows who.

Wrestling the place,
wrestling the time,
wrestling the matter.

Wrestling until dawn
calls shadow home.

The dark and the light
never fight about it.

And sometimes a sacred wound,
Jacob to Israel,
displaced and un-named,
one other into a thing,
happens after a night

wrestling with
   what knows who.

DAVID BREEDEN

PRAYERS AND DREAMINGS

With a bow to Ysaye Barnwell and Stephanie Kaza

Spirit within all, mysterious force giving shape to
    life, miraculous source and river of being,
help us to know who we are, to see our place in the
    history of the earth and in the family of things;
help us to see that we are part of all that ever was—
our grandmother's prayers and our grandfather's dreamings,
our mother's courage and our father's hope.

In our bones lies the calcium of antediluvian
    creatures,
in our veins courses the water of seas;
we are part of all that ever was,
born of this earth, riders upon a cosmic ocean;
we are not separate from nature, we are nature,
part of that same spirit that turned scales into
    feathers and birdsong into speech;
we live by the sun; we move by the stars . . .
we eat from the earth; we drink from the rain.

O great spirit, help us know who we are
and fill us with such love for this holy creation
and gratitude for this awesome gift we call living,

that we might claim our inheritance and live out
  our calling
to bless the world and each other with our care.

Amen

BECKY EDMISTON-LANGE

*The italicized lines quote the works of Ysaye Barnwell and
Stephanie Kaza, respectively.*

TWO LOVERS

It's October, not April, May, or June—those months usually associated with romance. There are few if any October love songs. Someone needs to write some, for that season of the year and for that season of life. True lovers know that love and romance can begin or last not only into or beyond October, but right up to the last minute of the last day in the December of life.

I saw two autumn lovers recently. He was in his seventies, she about the same. Their lovers' lane was a hospital cafeteria. I watched their love-making without embarrassment, for its unfolding was not immediately apparent and not at all sordid.

He set his tray down at the end of a long table and walked around to where she had set hers down. Slowly, gently, and with a slight shake in his hands, he pulled out the chair she was about to sit in. As he pushed it in, she sat. Then she followed him with her eyes as he retrieved his tray and placed it across from her. As he started to set his tray down, she gently rose just enough to place a steadying hand on the tray. Trays in place, silver in hand, they started to eat, speaking to one another softly.

There they were: truly lovely lovers. No, they weren't clutching or grabbing. They weren't billing or cooing. They weren't even kissing. Their loving looks, gestures, actions aren't the type seen on movie posters. Singles ads which speak of "moonlit walks by a lake," hardly touch the surface of what I saw. Their tenderness was much more seasoned and much more real. The moment spoke of years and a depth of true passion. Tears came to me and I turned away as any decent person should in the presence of those making love.

JOHN CORRADO

AUTUMN

the swirling colors of autumn surround us
glorious gold, yellow, and orange
bronzy brown, deep vibrant red
how can we not feel amazed and grateful?
here in our front row seats, watching
the rhythm of the changing seasons
the never-ending cycle of birth, growth, change, death

death in turn making ready
for new life

just for this moment
let me be still
let me rest
in the quiet of this sacred place
in the presence of the spirit gathered
held gently, yet mightily, by the threads of love
that bind us together

may whatever pain or sorrow or loss I feel today
be eased
if only for this moment
even as I feel tossed and turned by the wind
a fallen leaf, blown about
with no seeming direction
may I abandon the illusion of control
if only for this moment

and sense the love surrounding me
and the strength of the love within me

in reaching out
to receive and
in reaching out
to give back
may I bear witness
to love
may I bear witness
to life

ANN WILLEVER

MEDITATION ON OPPOSITES

Spirit of the universe,
Life force that flows through all beings,
Power beyond our knowing,

We ask you to help us see beyond our dependence
    on opposites—
To transcend our desire to know who is like us, and
    who is not.

Open us to the knowledge that in this room
there are complexities and diversities of identities
beyond black and white,
old and young,
woman and man,
poor and rich,
uneducated and educated,
disabled and able-bodied,
gay and straight,
ill and healthy,
wrong and right,
broken and whole.

In this room there are people who embody
    juxtaposition,
who can tell stories written on their bodies about
    both and *neither,*
who carry intimate pieces of the truth that there is

no such thing
as opposites.

Spirit of many names and of no name at all,
Help us find release from our belief that all things
    must be either/or,
this belief that walls us off from one another,
ensnaring us in a battle of same versus different.

Help us to open our minds,
to deeply listen,
and to truly know one another,
finally glimpsing the kaleidoscopic beauty of the
    divine.

ALEX KAPITAN

MAGICAL THINKING

The sign in the windowpane of Kristin Baybar's toy-shop in London reads, "We do not exist, but if you think we do and would like to visit . . . please knock." Knock I have. It is a strange and magical place, filled with curios, doll house furniture and hand-carved toys. Every surface is covered, the cupboard display cases stacked high, with miniature flowers, snapping tin alligators, painted puzzles that move, penny whistles, and cheap magic tricks. Signs proclaiming "Do Not Touch" suggest that this might not be a shop for small children.

Yet some of my fondest childhood memories are of Kristin Baybar's. For three summers, while my father taught a study abroad course, my family rented a flat around the corner. Every chance I got I wandered over to the toy shop. The shop owner seemed to delight in entertaining small children. There were magic tricks, toys that made noises, and puzzles.

The shop and its owner taught me about the power of the imagination. Creative play, the ability to dream and discover new things helps make us human. Without them there would be no culture, no religion, no art, and no science. They help us to define and redefine the world, for as William Shakespeare wrote, "We are such stuff / As dreams are made."

My friend Richard defined magic as the act of imagining something and then creating it. He would say, "I think, 'I'm hungry. I want a sandwich.' I imagine it and then I create it. That's magic!" Open yourself to the marvelous that surrounds you, seek it out, if only for a moment, and you never know what sort of magic you might create. So much of the world began as a dream. So much of the world has yet to be dreamed.

COLIN BOSSEN

NOVEMBER

Almost but not quite here
the cold and dark of winter
hovers on the wings of early dusk
and in the pale dark chill
of mornings late in coming.

The gleaners with their baskets
gone
the fields of gold-brown stubble in the waning light
stretch out with nothing
left.

Naked trees
stripped of their secrets
shiver in restless wind
make noisy lace against the pewter sky.

There is a cold spare elegance
in this uncluttered emptiness
of stone and rock and branch and tree
no charming artifice of leaf and flower
no budding fruits
no shining hour
no scent of sun-warmed pines
on forest floor
no musty tang of mushrooms
in a rotten log.

And yet
there is a vital honesty
in this bare simplicity
God dwells here
in even the darkest shadows.

While some chase the sun
all we need do
is keep on looking.

JUDITH CAMPBELL

A CALM, CLEAR PLACE

Let us come into a calm, clear place
Where we can relinquish our clutter
And relax from busyness into being.

Let us settle into that calm, clear place
Where the earth supports our bodies
And the community lifts our spirits,
Where we can breathe in peace
And center ourselves in love.

Let us welcome our calm, clear place
Where our hearts can open
And our thoughts can expand
Beyond the cobwebs of convention
Into the creative flow of infinity.

JEZIBELL ANAT

GOD HAS NO BORDERS

We humans are the line-drawers. We are the border-makers. We are the boundary-testers. We are the census-takers. We draw a line to separate this from that, so we can see clearly what each is. We create a border to define our place, so we can take care of what's there. We test boundaries to find if they are real, if they are necessary, if they are just. We congregate within those boundaries in families and tribes and cities and countries that we call *us*. And we call people on the other side *them*.

But our minds seek boundaries that our hearts know not. The lines we draw disappear when viewed with eyes of compassion. The recognition of human kinship does not end at any border. A wiser part of us knows that the other is us, and we them.

Let justice flow like water and peace like a never-ending stream. Let compassion glow like sunlight and love like an ever-shining beam. The rain, the sunshine, the breeze, the life-giving air we breathe—they know no boundaries. Neither do our empathy, our good will, our concern for one another.

God has no borders. Love has no borders. Let us lift up the awareness of our unity as we celebrate our awesome diversity on this beautiful day.

ROD RICHARDS

PRAYER

Spirit of Life that Abounds and Surrounds Us
as we walk our individual paths
in our individual worlds
at our individual pace
we have all been led here this morning
to this convocation of human spirits
where we can revel in each other's light
where we can share, *compartir,* just how similar
our "individual" paths seem
in a world that reflects back
the negativity of difference.

Thank you for your patience
as we roam in circles
searching, searching
for the hand that we do not notice right beside us
or the face full of love and devotion
that we do not recognize as our own.

Spirit of This World and Beyond
we strive to keep conscious
our interconnections,
our interdependence,
our trust in one another as humans *being*
humans
being
loving

being
in truth and with compassion
for we know

that what we send out to the universe
is what will return
and we wish to send our love
to restore this broken world.

MARTA I. VALENTÍN

GLORY TRANSFORMED

November has blown the Autumn down.
Leaves, whipped from the trees
by wind and rain
shine in rain-slicked piles,
float in ponds and puddles,
blow along the curb sides
and muffle the earth.

Crimson and gold gone now
to dun and brown
and branches lift black hands
naked to the sky.

Glory is changed, but it is not undone.
Under the mantle of death and decay,
life turns again in its hidden dance.
Leaves shed of brilliance sink into themselves,
dissolved and coaxed to a new becoming.
Unsung, without notice, through winter darkness
they nourish the roots and then they rise,
cell to filament, to bark, branch and bud,
pulled to new form by the warming air.

The lesson is murmured there beneath our feet:
  some glory is humble and hidden from sight,
  there is nurture and solace in unlikely form
  and the weaving flow leaves nothing behind—
life and death into life, everlasting.

KATHLEEN McTIGUE

PREPARING FOR A HIKE

consider the season
    in the spring, pack sandals for water crossings
    in the fall, a space blanket for the unplanned
        night out

consider the route
    imagine your way through the good route
    and also the other route, the less preferred,
    the one you'll need when the first proves
        impassable

consider what to carry in your head
    don't listen to sappy music before setting off
    the sappier the music
    the more you will resent your own brain
    don't worry about what to do with your head
    your head won't work after some hours on
        the trail

consider what you'll pass through
    know your trees, your ferns, your mushrooms,
    know your wild flowers, both the garish and
        the shy,
    know the birds by their calls,
    and distinguish the chickadee from the white-
        throated sparrow
    mind the oven bird

take joy in the winter wren,
your most tireless companion

and be ready, with the first step,
to give up control
and let the journey unfold on its own,
as it most certainly will.

let its accidents become opportunities,
let its challenges become triumphs,
let it enter your heart and inhabit you,
let it sanctify you,
let you and the journey and nature be one,

as you most certainly are.

JOHN MERCER

WHAT I KNOW

I do not know where we go when we die;
And I do not know what the soul is
Or what death is or when or why.

What I know is that
The song once sung cannot be unsung,
And the life once lived cannot be unlived,
And the love once loved cannot be unloved.

KENNETH COLLIER

HIDDEN IN THE HEART

Hidden in the heart
of late autumn's barren
fields is the ripening
of seasons yet to come.
Roots clinging to frozen ground
wait patiently
for their next long drink.
Seeds fallen from last summer's blooms
sleep beneath blankets of quilted leaves
and feathered snow.

Fruits of the future,
words unripened into speech,
truth present but unseen,
evidence yet to be awakened
by the faithful
unfolding
of time and love.

KAREN HERING

GO BOLDLY

May you be brave enough to expose
your aching woundedness
and reveal your vulnerability.

May you speak your deepest truths,
knowing that they will change as you do.

May you sing the music within you,
composing your own melody,
playing your song with all your heart.

May you draw, paint, sculpt, and sew,
showing the world your vision.

May you write letters, poetry, biography,
slogans, graffiti, the great novel,
laying bare your words to love and hate.

May you love even though your heart
breaks again and again.

And until the end of your days,
may your life be filled
with possibilities and courage.

JEAN M. OLSON

MY MOTHER THE SCULPTOR

She gouges, chips, sands. And
there the great head, his lips,
his big infectious laugh,
his always gesturing hands.

Each log becomes a part
of who she is and who
he is. Married so many
years before he faded away.

In another log she finds
the lovers entwined. Wooden
arms and torsos transform
to embracing passionate flesh.

Now in a smaller piece,
he is much older, lowered eyes,
lips sad, longing for, but not
understanding, what he has lost.

But she understands and carves
and knows her loss. She
finishes this piece, then
puts her tools, finally, away.

JOAN McINTOSH

THE DEER

You must stand perfectly still
and look like a very peculiar tree.
And if you move, it must look like
it was the wind that blew your hand
to your face. And the deer will look
right back at you without moving their tails.
They will look, and you will think that maybe
they are not really there. But then, they will
move their ears, and you will know they are real.

And that is what it is like.
It is like the sweet, almost immovable deer.
It sounds green, like rain falling through leaves.
It sounds blue, like wind across the bay and the sea.
It sounds silver and black, like the sky
when there is nothing left of the day
but sleep and soft sounds
of breathing and dreams that drift upward
like smoke and disappear.

It moves as slowly and carefully
as a heron stepping deliberately
through the still water of the pond.
And it is almost silent. Almost.
Not quite. Silent like the falling snow
is silent. It whispers against the window,
or sings, or even hisses like a fire
made of apple wood hisses.

Or maybe you won't know it is there
until it stops. Until the whispering is hushed.
Maybe you won't know it is there until
it is not there. And then you will long for it
to return. Oh, you will long for it,
like the dry grass longs for the rain.
And all you can do is be still and wait.

But do not worry. And do not hurry.
For the clouds will gather eventually
and the rain will fall with a rattle into the grass.
The whisper will return like the deer that moved
its ear and you will sigh a long, sweet sigh.
And know that it is there.

The throaty sound of knowledge,
the sudden splash of understanding,
washes over you like a waterfall, like starlight,
like a dream that makes the day come alive.
And you will know it in the little daily things:
the smell of coffee, the touch of hands,
the sound of light falling on grass,
the taste of air after rain.
You will know it and never forget.

But maybe you ask, "What is this thing?
What is it that moves as silently as snow?"

And what shall I answer? It is nothing but the deer.

KENNETH COLLIER

BENEDICTION

Let us go in the spirit of love,
never knowing when or where we may find the divine,
yet conscious of the spark within each of us,
and the unfolding beauty that surrounds us.

Let us go in peace.
Let us go in love.
May our lives be a blessing.
Amen.

COLIN BOSSEN

Unitarians and Universalists have been publishing prayer collections and meditation manuals for more than 170 years. In 1841 the Unitarians broke with their tradition of addressing only theological topics and published *Short Prayers for the Morning and Evening of Every Day in the Week, with Occasional Prayers and Thanksgivings.* Over the years, the Unitarians published many more volumes of prayers, including Theodore Parker's selections. In 1938 *Gaining a Radiant Faith* by Henry H. Saunderson launched the tradition of an annual Lenten manual.

Several Universalist collections appeared in the early nineteenth century. A comprehensive Book of Prayers was published in 1839, featuring both public and private devotions. Like the Unitarians, the Universalists published Lenten manuals, and in the 1950s they complemented this series with Advent manuals.

Since 1961, the year the Unitarians and Universalists consolidated, the Lenten manual has evolved into a meditation manual.

For a complete list of meditation manuals, please visit
www.uua.org/skinner/meditation